Original Title: Whispers in Meditation

Copyright © 2023 Book Fairy Publishing
All rights reserved.

Editors: Theodor Taimla
Autor: Annabel Swan
ISBN 978-9916-39-441-0

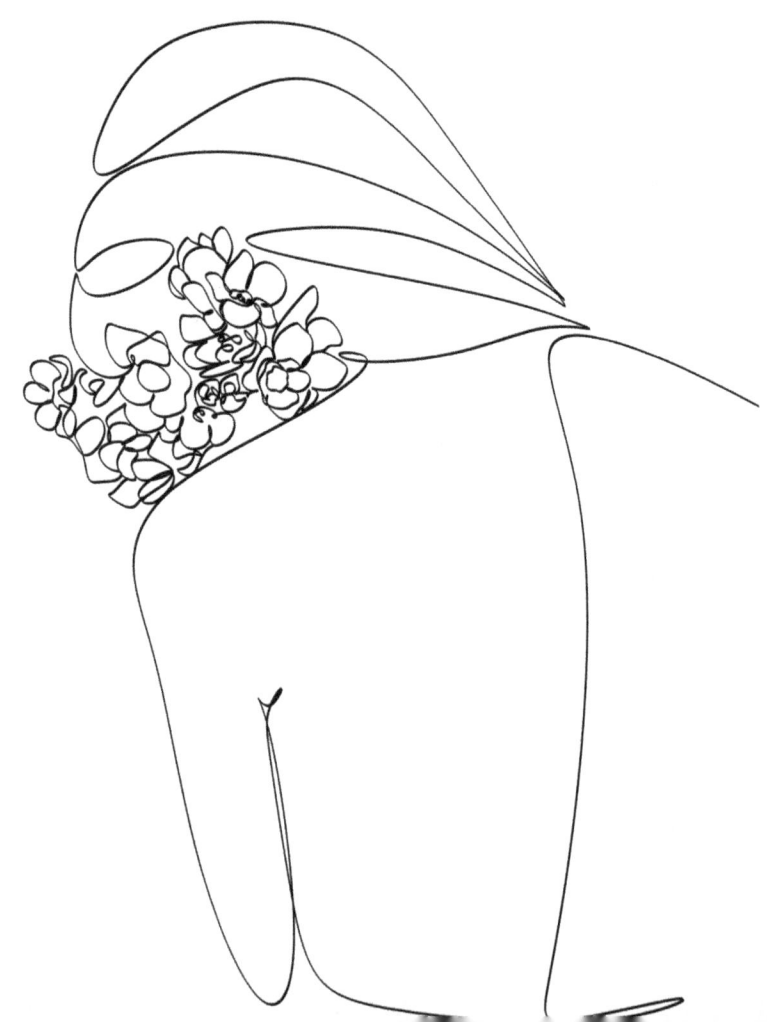

The Humble Voice of Introspection

Inside myself, I softly tread,
To hear the words my spirit said.
A muted voice, not often heard,
Speaks with wisdom, undeterred.

Through the heart's reflective glass,
I view the echoes of the past.
Each memory, both sweet and sore,
A lesson learned, an open door.

In quietude, I seek the truth,
Of youth's bravado, age's ruth.
The humble voice, an internal guide,
Within its counsel, I confide.

The Muted Melody of Mindfulness

In silence, soft and soundless sway,
Beneath the noise, a quiet lay.
Breaths rise and fall, a gentle tide,
In mindful peace, our thoughts abide.

Within the soul's hushed inner room,
Where silence blooms and insights loom.
Past currents rush, but here inside,
The muted melody does bide.

A tranquil hum, a whisper light,
A dance of being, pure and right.
Mind's eye opens, casting shade,
On tumult's storm, until it's frayed.

Thought's Tender Whistle

In mind's vast sky, a whistle blows,
A tender thought so faintly glows.
It drifts aloft on zephyrs mild,
An echo of the inner child.

Each gentle puff, a soft refrain,
That sings of joy, and soothes the pain.
A ballad wrought from deep within,
On breath's light wing, it twirls and spins.

This tender tune the heart does cradle,
As stars above in night's dome twinkle.
Resounding through the soul's vast halls,
Where whispers rise and shadow falls.

Murmurs Beneath Serenity's Surface

Below the calm, a whisper stirs,
A murmur soft, serenity blurs.
It trickles through the still mind's lake,
Where thoughts are deep, but never break.

A gentle rustle, trees of thought,
The sound of calmness, sweetly wrought.
The underlying silent chant,
Where secrets dwell, but never daunt.

Though placid waters show no trace,
Below, the murmurs interlace.
Subdued, they weave through strands of peace,
In unseen depths, they never cease.

Stirring Stillness

Amidst the still, a stirring breeze,
A shiver through the tranquil trees.
The stillness moves, begins to twist,
A silent dance of morning mist.

It whispers soft to every blade,
The stillness stirred, but not betrayed.
Within the calm, a pulse awakes,
A subtle shift, the dawn remakes.

The world in motion, quiet, sly,
Below the ever-waking sky.
The hush is full, yet speaks of more,
In stirring stillness, life's encore.

Light Whispers of Inner Harmony

In quietude, a gentle light does gleam,
Within the soul, a tranquil river flows.
A whisper soft as morning mist on streams,
Inner harmony in silence grows.

The heart's soft beat beneath still chest does hum,
Life's ebbing cares all quelled, serenely calm.
Breaths weave the tapestry where peace comes from,
In warmth of inner light, a healing balm.

With every pulse, the light flares bright and true,
Diffusing through the shadows of the mind.
A luminescent dance of subtle hue,
Whispers of warmth, to which our cores align.

The final notes of day's soft symphony,
Within each resting thought, find sanctity.

Faded Murmurings of Focus

The murmurings of focus softly fade,
Like ink-dipped quill that scrawls across a page.
The mindful siege on scattered thoughts is laid,
Within this moment, mind and breath engage.

Forgotten whispers, focus now reclaimed,
A vigil kept o'er vast and endless sea.
The currents of distraction now are tamed,
In mental fortress of tranquility.

With every breath, the faded murmurs wane,
A softened echo in the chambered thought.
Intent's sharp edge cuts through the mental grain,
To carve from chaos the serenity sought.

Within the fortress walls, such focus lies,
A silent strength beneath the closing skies.

Sibilant Sounds of the Sublime

The sibilant sounds of the resplendent sublime,
A symphony serenely swimming in time.
Each sussuration sweeps the soul to climb,
A journey's ascent, in rhythm and rhyme.

Soothing whispers sing through the silent air,
A chorus of calmness, a soft-spoken prayer.
The world's sharp noises, now rendered bare,
A sigh of the wind, a silence rare.

Ethereal echoes glide gracefully by,
Sublime in their sussuration, under the sky.
The harmony holds, as if to defy,
The turbulence of life, without need to try.

And in that sibilant, whispering sound,
The essence of peace, profoundly found.

Undertones of the Meditative Mind

Beneath the bustle, undertones arise,
A quiet cadence of the meditative mind.
In depths of thought, a silent refuge lies,
An inner sanctum, peacefully aligned.

The world outside, a distant, muffled drum,
Its rhythm soft against the mind's gentle hum.
The undertones, a soothing pulse become,
A mantra's murmur, simply spoken, 'om'.

Amidst the noise, we seek the soundless score,
The tranquil timbre of thought's deepest core.
A resonance that renders rich the poor,
In contemplation, opens hidden door.

These undertones that in silence abound,
In depths of stillness, profound truths are found.

Echoes of the Inner Voice

Whispers creep from silent lips,
Echoing in the soul's eclipse,
Each murmur a hidden confession,
A narrative in silent progression.

A shiver of truth in the quiet dusk,
Inner dialogues in twilight musk,
Voices from within, faintly heard,
In the heart, every silent word.

Chambers deep where secrets dwell,
Soul's stories that yearn to tell,
Echoes of thoughts yet to be spoken,
Keys to doors that remain unbroken.

A symphony played without a sound,
Where the self and truth are bound,
Inward echoes that guide the way,
Illuminating our inner fray.

Murmurs of the Mindful Breeze

Gentle gusts of knowing air,
Carry thoughts too soft to declare,
A tender touch upon the cheek,
Murmurs of the breeze that speak.

Leaves that dance to silent tunes,
Rhythmic rustles in calm afternoons,
A voice that travels through the trees,
Whispering secrets with mindful ease.

An ancient wisdom on the wing,
Airborne wisdom that zephyrs bring,
Softly speaking to hearts that heed,
The subtle murmur of nature's creed.

Carried aloft in the open skies,
Nature's breath, soulful and wise,
Speaking to those who choose to listen,
In every gentle breeze that glistens.

Hushed Tones of Tranquility

In stillness deep, the world recedes,
And tranquil thoughts the quiet heeds,
Softly spoken in mind's embrace,
In hushed tones, find the solace.

A sanctuary of silent sound,
Where peace and serenity abound,
Whispered calm in each breath drawn,
Nature's lullaby until dawn.

Gentle echoes in the silent room,
Balance the mind, dispel the gloom,
Harmony found in the quietude's nest,
Hushed tones that lull to rest.

The world outside fades away,
Serenity whispers and holds sway,
Gently the heart finds its equanimity,
Cradled in hushed tones of tranquility.

Silent Chants of Serenity

Inaudible psalms of peaceful bliss,
Serenity's breath, a silent kiss,
Chanting softly without a voice,
In the quietude, we rejoice.

Sonic threads woven in the air,
Crafting a tapestry of care,
Silent mantras that resonate,
In whispered tones, they alleviate.

Vibrations felt, not heard or seen,
Calm cadences, pure and serene,
Melodies in mute refrain,
Chants of silence to sustain.

Within the stillness, find reprieve,
Where silent songs weave and interweave,
In every chant, contentment's key,
Velvet silence, tranquility's plea.

Gentle Gestures of the Spirit

In whispers of the rustling leaves,
A gentle spirit sighs,
It wanders through the silent eves,
And in the stillness, lies.

Touching hearts with tender care,
Its breath a soothing hymn,
In moments soft as evening air,
The world feels far less grim.

The dance of light on rippling streams,
In nature's cradle slept,
The spirit moves within our dreams,
And promises it kept.

Through acts of kindness, small but sure,
Its presence we observe,
With every gentle gesture pure,
It serves to calm and nerve.

Mind's Silent Sirens

In the deep ocean of the mind,
Silent sirens sing their tales,
Of thoughts unmoored, and dreams entwined,
Where logic often fails.

Their songs echo in hidden caves,
In corridors untouched by light,
Pulling at the anchors in waves,
And steering ships through the night.

These sirens, with their haunting tones,
Blend truth with sweet deceit,
Challenging the mind's uncharted zones,
Where fear and longing meet.

Beneath the surface, hear their call,
A symphony of the soul's sea,
In the mind's deep, they enthrall,
Singing of what could be.

Essence of the Unspoken

There is an essence unspoken, it dwells,
Beyond the realm of words, it swells,
In every pause and silence held,
A universe of meaning, spelled.

It's in the glance that lovers share,
In the quiet comfort of a stare,
The language deep within their eyes,
Speaks volumes without a guise.

Between the lines of what we say,
Lies a truth that won't decay,
The heartfelt secrets we consign,
In the essence that's divine.

In every breath of wind that passed,
In connections that forever last,
The unspoken finds its voice,
And through our bonds, it will rejoice.

Tranquility's Undercurrent

Beneath the surface tumult, peace,
Where clarity and calm increase,
An undercurrent still and deep,
Where tranquil waters lull to sleep.

Even as the storms above rage on,
Below, serenity is never gone,
In unseen depths, it flows serene,
A silent strength, felt yet unseen.

To find this peace, one must dive within,
Past the noise, and life's loud din,
In quietude, the heart will find,
The tranquil balm for ruffled mind.

So listen for that gentle flow,
The undercurrent, soft and slow,
It whispers reassurance, so clear,
In every quiet breath, it's near.

Whispers of Inner Peace

In the quiet of dawn's soft embrace,
Gentle whispers stir the silent space.
Echoes of warmth, a tender trace,
Calm serenity on life's hectic race.

Beneath the tumult, a soothing tide,
Inner peace where true thoughts reside.
A reservoir deep, where anxieties hide,
In this sanctuary, worries subside.

Calm breaths in, the world fades out,
The whispers of peace quiet the shout.
In the heart's core, devoid of doubt,
A tranquil flame, eternally stout.

Whispers guide to the hushed retreat,
Where self and serenity sweetly meet.
Each moment savored, so complete,
In inner peace, we're truly replete.

Tranquil Mind's Soft Call

Hark, the tranquil mind doth softly call,
    Beneath the din, beneath the brawl.
A whispering wind through autumn's fall,
    A stillness waiting to enthrall.

Through the rustling leaves of time's own tree,
    A melody hums, sets the spirit free.
    All chaos fades, just calm and me,
The soft call echoes, 'come and see'.

In the gentle hush of morning's light,
    Clarity sings, and all feels right.
A tranquil mind takes its placid flight,
    Above the earth, beyond the night.

    The call, a balm to every woe,
    In its quietude, we come to know.
    With every breath, serenity grows,
In tranquil mind, life's beauty shows.

Contemplation's Gentle Nudge

Contemplation knocks with gentle nudge,
Whispering secrets, it won't begrudge.
Reflective moments we trudge,
Emerging wise, without a judge.

Ideas form like morning dew,
Each a lens, granting a new view.
The inner eye seeks what's true,
In silent thought, insights accrue.

A pondered pause, life's busy stage,
Turning inward, the sage's page.
Each silent thought a timeless sage,
Wisdom unlocked, the soul's wage.

From this quiet, a world reframed,
No longer chaos, no longer blamed.
In calmness born, life reclaimed,
By contemplation's nudge, we're named.

Silenced Musings

In the realm where thoughts lay bare,
Silenced musings take the chair.
No spoken words disrupt the air,
Just hushed reflections to declare.

The silence speaks more than sound,
In its depth, lost truths are found.
A hallowed space, a sacred ground,
Mind's musings, the only resound.

Whispered secrets in the mind's ear,
Not to be shouted, but to hear.
Within the quiet, they appear,
Silenced thoughts, oh so clear.

So in the silent interlude,
Let not the silence be misconstrued.
It's in the hush, wisdom's pursued,
In quieted thought, life is renewed.

Unheard Utterings

In quiet corners of my mind,
Where thoughts like whispers tend to bind,
The subtle sounds of heart we find,
In solitude, remain confined.

Words not spoken, nor defined,
Ponderings of the deepest kind,
Secrets with their threads entwined,
Silent echoes left unsigned.

These unheard utterings of the soul,
A soft lament that takes its toll,
In silent chamber's hidden role,
They shape me, quiet, make me whole.

Ghosts of phrases never told,
Ideas against the mold,
In the stillness, they unfold,
Unheard stories, brave and bold.

The Subtle Susurrus of Self

A whisper winds within the will,
A gentle gust, a quiet thrill,
The self it speaks in voice so still,
In inner space, it does instill.

With every sigh, with every hush,
Streams of silent thoughts do gush,
Beneath the noise, a tranquil crush,
The subtle susurrus does flush.

It's in the pause, the break, the rest,
Where subtleties are oft expressed,
Within, the words are softly dressed,
In silence, where they manifest.

This inner voice, not brash, but fleet,
In echoes of the heart does greet,
Not loud, but in the calm, replete,
The whispering self does so entreat.

Inward Murmurings

The murmurings of mind within,
Hushed tones of what might have been,
The sotto voce thoughts begin,
To paint the soul with wordless din.

In chambers deep where dreams are spun,
Where fears and hopes in dance are one,
The murmurs weigh a ton or none,
And speak in tongues of the undone.

Inward murmurings that sing,
Of love and loss, and everything,
They pluck at psyche's tender string,
In soundless serenade, they cling.

Whispers of the inner tide,
Of timid truth that seeks to hide,
The sighs that dwell in shadows wide,
Within, where secret musings bide.

Undertones of Deep Calm

Below the tempest's wild uproar,
In depths where peace begins to pour,
The undertones of calm restore,
Balance to the core.

Beneath life's heaving, surging swarm,
The quiet holds a potent form,
A steady stream, a tranquil norm,
Where stillness weathers storm.

In gentle waves of silent balm,
Lies strength beneath the outward qualm,
A realm where flustered thoughts embalm,
In depths of deep, deep calm.

So let the surface churn and spin,
While underneath, where sights are dim,
Soft undertones do so begin,
To sing life's placid hymn.

Secret Susurrations of the Spirit

In depths of silence, secrets sway,
A gentle rustle, spirits play.
Amidst the quietness, they twine,
In whispers only hearts define.

Echoes of an inner dance,
Murmurings that barely prance.
Through the soul's veiled corridor,
Sacred secrets to explore.

A breath of thought, so softly heard,
In the space where words are blurred.
Spirits speak in tender tones,
In confessions, the silence owns.

Subtle stirring in the chest,
Where all the hidden truths are dressed.
The spirit's code, a silent speech,
In silent susurrations, reach.

Muted Words of the Wise

Weights of wisdom, softly tread,
Words unspoken, thoughts unsaid.
In the muted pause between,
Lies the knowledge seldom seen.

Eyes that speak when lips are still,
The sage's glance, the quiet thrill.
Gestures teaching without sound,
Where the depths of truth are found.

A nod, a wink, a gentle stare,
Wisdom's whispers fill the air.
Silent dialogues they weave,
In the threads we scarce perceive.

Learned in moments still as stone,
Messages through stillness shown.
The wise convey with rests and space,
The power in the mute embrace.

Inward Whispers of Wandering Thoughts

Through the catacombs of mind,
Where the thoughts meander, blind.
A soft echo, a ripple's breath,
An inward whisper, quiet as death.

Stray fragments of ideas rove,
In the labyrinth of the trove.
Wandering whispers are the seeds,
Of the garden that never bleeds.

Conversations with the self,
On the dusty, mental shelf.
Where thoughts, like spiders, spin and weave,
In the tapestry that they conceive.

Solitary murmurings sway,
In the chambers of clay.
Thoughts that in solitude bloom,
With whispers that fill the room.

Pensive Humming of the Conscious

In stillness rings a thoughtful hum,
Of conscious streams that slowly come.
Pensive tones that resonate,
Within the mind to cogitate.

A melody of thought and plight,
That hums throughout the day and night.
It's the vibration of the known,
In the pitch that's solely our own.

The rhythm of reflection deep,
In the soul's own music, steep.
A hum of pensive pace and poise,
A silent score, the heart's own voice.

Humming in the thoughtful brain,
The conscious dance, the quiet strain.
A tune that carries hopes and fears,
The music of our inner spheres.

Undertalk of the Unconscious

Beneath the cloak of consciousness,
A whispered undertalk prevails,
In sleeping depths, it softly walks,
On shadowed paths, it never fails.

A language formed of dreams and signs,
Its dialogue is never heard,
Yet in its grip, the secrets bind,
And speak in silence, without words.

Unseen emotions hold discourse,
In realms untamed by waking mind,
Where psyche's voice finds primal source,
And truths unwind, uniquely kind.

The inner talk of souls at rest,
An undercurrent deep and vast,
Reveals what often goes unguessed,
In silent speech, the die is cast.

Wherewithal in the Wordless

Within the silent, wordless spaces,
Resides a force, unseen, yet strong,
A wherewithal that time embraces,
In quietude, where hearts belong.

It speaks in pauses and in glances,
A language felt, but never heard,
In wordless depths, the soul advances,
The speechless strength in action stirred.

A presence in the gaps of chatter,
Where meaning lies in what's not said,
In stillness, finds what truly matters,
Beyond the noise, our spirits fed.

The wordless weave their silent stories,
In threads of life's enduring dance,
In hush, we find the fleeting glories,
And in the quiet, life's expanse.

Oscillations in the Oasis of Peace

Within the tranquil oasis calm,
Life's oscillations softly hum,
A symphony in whispered psalm,
Where peace and restful hearts succumb.

The pendulum of time swings slow,
In rhythm with the breath of trees,
Here moments meld and gently flow,
In sync with nature's silent ease.

The ebb and flow of silent thought,
Within this refuge finds its pace,
In solace, all that's sought is caught,
In gentle arms of time's embrace.

Amidst the stillness, motion stirs,
A dance of peace, both old and new,
In whispers where the soul concurs,
In restful shades of verdant hue.

Unspoken Understandings Unraveled

There lies a world of unspoke lore,
Where understandings weave their thread,
No need for words to say much more,
In silent nods, much is said.

An unvoiced pact 'tween kindred souls,
In glances, much is understood,
The gap where silent comfort rolls,
Where words fall short, silence should.

The tacit tales of eyes that speak,
In volumes loud, yet hushed and low,
In gazing deep, no need to seek,
For in the unsaid, friendships grow.

In quietude, we come to find,
The language of the heart's own sound,
Unraveled thoughts of like-mind bind,
Where peace and kinship are profound.

Secrets of the Inner Mind

In the maze of thoughts untold,
Deep where secrets dare unfold,
Whispers in the chambers blind,
Treasures of the inner mind.

A vault of dreams in quiet guise,
Holding echoes of silent cries,
Unfathomed truths that we may find,
In the vast expanse of the conscious mind.

Layers upon layers deeply twine,
Each one a story, a unique design,
In this abyss where thoughts are mined,
Lie the secrets of the inner mind.

A garden of fears, worries combined,
Where hope and despair are entwined,
In the quietude, solace we find,
Embracing the secrets of the inner mind.

Hushed Voices Within

There's a whispering, a subtle din,
From the hushed voices held within,
They speak of love, of loss, of sin,
An inner dialogue that never thins.

Through the heart's corridors, they begin,
A symphony, a violin,
Playing tunes of what's been,
Hushed voices within, ever so thin.

In every silence, they chime in,
Words unspoken, they're akin,
To ghosts of past, or next of kin,
The hushed voices within do spin.

They are the echoes, the soul's tailspin,
The murmurs of what could have been,
They are our thoughts, wearing thin,
The hushed voices within, softly akin.

Gentle Murmurs of the Soul

In quiet moments, soft and droll,
The heart converses with the soul,
A gentle murmur, a quiet stroll,
Through a world that makes us whole.

Beneath the chaos, beyond control,
Lies a rhythm, a gentle scroll,
Whispering tales of a distant goal,
The gentle murmurs of the soul.

They speak of joy, a blooming knoll,
Of healing wounds, of making whole,
In whispers that seem to cajole,
The gentle murmurs of the soul.

A stream of wisdom, a mindful toll,
Conversations without a dole,
In our essence, they pay the toll,
The gentle murmurs of the soul.

Silent Chants of Reflection

In moments still, beneath the shoal,
Where thoughts and silence gently bowl,
There resonate a pure patrol,
Silent chants of the reflection's goal.

Beyond the noise, a hidden poll,
Thoughts appraising their own role,
In the silence, there's a console,
Silent chants of reflection unroll.

Threading through the heart's loophole,
A dialogue without extol,
Meditative words, a monopole,
Silent chants of reflection extol.

Mind's orchestra, a tranquil shoal,
Forming a serene aureole,
Amidst life's play, a sacred stole,
Silent chants of reflection, the soul.

The Psychic's Quiet Parlance

In a room where whispers thread the air,
Echoing secrets from who knows where,
A psychic gazes through time's wide lens,
With words unspoken the silence bends.

Mysteries dance in a quiet trance,
Future and past in her mind advance,
She reads the story in a silent glance,
In the parlance of the psychic's stance.

Visions summoned in hushed repose,
As the cosmos its knowledge bestows,
Silent words that no one else knows,
In the quiet, her insight grows.

The aura's hues softly disclose,
Tales untold that the heart enclose,
Softly spoken in mental prose,
This quiet parlance gracefully flows.

Dialogue with the Divine Hush

Amidst the calm, a sacred sigh,
Conversations that souls imply,
With the divine, a silent cry,
Beneath the hush of the sky-high.

In stillness lies the profound talk,
Where spirits gather and angels walk,
Every thought becomes a silent squawk,
In the divine hush where we intersect and balk.

Whispers of the heavens, subtly caught,
In the muteness, profound thoughts are wrought,
In quietude, wisdom is sought,
The divine dialogue in silent thought.

The hallowed quiet, a wordless tutor,
In the silence, faith is the suitor,
In every mute moment, the divine rooter,
Through silence, becomes life's astute commuter.

Subtle Stirrings in the Silence

In the hush, a quiver begins,
A soft rustling against the quiet's skins,
Subtle stirrings awaken the dins,
Where silence starts and where it thins.

Gentle murmurs of life's rebirth,
Whispers of the wind, fleeting mirth,
Silence is filled with unvoiced girth,
Embracing the stories untold on Earth.

In stillness, beating hearts converse,
Silent interplay, universe to universe,
Each pulse a stanza, each breath a verse,
In the silence, our essences immerse.

Quiet ripples across the mind's lake,
In each hush, a new awakening, awake,
Subtle stirrings for the soul to partake,
Within the silence, life's echoes shake.

The Unwhispered Words of Wisdom

Beneath the clamor, wisdom waits,
Silent knowing that time creates,
The unwhispered truths it contemplates,
In the quietude, enlightenment incubates.

Words unsaid, yet understood,
The language of the wise and good,
Unspoken knowledge in quietude stood,
The unwhispered wisdom of life's brotherhood.

In silent thought, insights bloom,
Beyond the noise, beyond the gloom,
In wisdom's garden, thoughts perfume,
In unvoiced depths, the truths resume.

The silent sagas of knowing eyes,
Where wisdom silent, never dies,
It whispers not, but still it tries,
Through unwhispered words, the sage implies.

Subtle Sounds of Solitude

In the hush where whispers dwell,
A silent orchestra does swell.
Nature breathes a solo tune,
Solitude's embrace 'neath the crescent moon.

Shadows dance without a sound,
Casting shapes upon the ground.
Thoughts like leaves, in breezes caught,
Carry weight, yet hold naught.

Streams of consciousness flow deep,
Through the mind's vast, endless sweep.
Every rustle, sigh, and hush,
Crafts a world in twilight's blush.

In the quiet, truth is found,
Where the self has no bound.
Echoes of a hidden place,
In the subtle sounds of solitude's grace.

Gentle Murmurings of the Soul

Amidst the noise, a gentle strain,
Whispers of the heart's refrain.
Murmurings soft, and bittersweet,
An inner rhythm, a tranquil beat.

It speaks in tongues of ancient lore,
In sighs that swell from the core.
A tender voice from deep within,
Whispering of where we've been.

A lullaby to the wounded parts,
Healing the cracks in broken hearts.
Gentle murmurs, soul's chime,
A timeless song, a rhyme sublime.

In quiet moments, it's heard the best,
When mind's at peace, the soul at rest.
In every man's own hallowed hall,
Listen—to the gentle murmurings of the soul.

Soft Echoes in Silence

Soft echoes drift in boundless space,
Silence speaks with tender grace.
A feather's fall, a breath's light trace,
A solemn tempo, nature's pace.

Quietude's cloak, a velvet might,
Envelops day, caresses night.
In the vacuum of the quiet,
Echoes bounce with secret riot.

In the stillness, echo's flight,
Casts to ears like beams of light.
Whispered secrets, nuanced tones,
In the pauses, meaning groans.

An unseen dance, an unheard part,
Resonating in the heart.
Soft echoes in silence rest,
In the quiet, they speak best.

Quiet Stirrings of the Heart

In the depth of night so stark,
Quiet stirrings of the heart.
A gentle nudge, a subtle start,
The feelings that new dreams impart.

A stirring soft, a flicker faint,
A canvas for the soul to paint.
The heart, it whispers, pulses, pleads,
Within one's chest, where hope seeds.

Emotions swirl, a silent storm,
Within the chest, they take form.
Desires unspoken, love's warm art,
Are quiet stirrings of the heart.

A murmur here, a wish there part,
Threads of silence deftly chart.
The silent orchestra does play,
Where heart's stirrings softly sway.

Inner Sanctum's Murmurs

In chambers deep where shadows dance,
the heart's soft whispers spin and lance.
Silent echos, a hushed refrain,
secrets swathed in the mind's domain.

In this haven, away from roar,
thoughts unfurl, inner core to explore.
Murmurs like a secret stream,
carry forth the subconscious dream.

Vibrations of a muted hum,
where fears and hopes together come.
With every pulsating surge,
Inner sanctum and self merge.

Within the silent sanctum's walls,
intuition quietly calls.
A sanctuary, pure and tacit,
housing the soul's most private facet.

Breath of the Quiet Mind

In stillness, breath draws a gentle arc,
quiet ripples in the dawn's soft dark.
The mind's clamor fades away,
as tranquil thoughts begin to sway.

Each inhale a brush with peace,
internal dialogues slowly cease.
Exhalation casts aside,
worries that in whispers hide.

The tranquil mind's steady stream,
filters light through a waking dream.
In the quiet, truth finds its voice,
giving rise to the mindful choice.

Breathing in serenity's light,
clearing mists that cloud the sight.
Within the calm, clarity's born,
as breath of quiet breaks the morn.

Solitude's Silent Symphony

Alone, where even echoes hide,
a symphony plays deep inside.
The notes, they hang in pensive air,
a quiet melody of the solitaire.

Each silence feeds the inner tune,
a cosmic dance with a silent moon.
The chords they resonate and bend,
in solitude, a trusted friend.

No audience, save for the mind,
whispers of the soul, unconfined.
In the hush, reflection hums,
to the beat of its own drums.

The silent symphony prevails,
as thought and stillness lift the veils.
Solitude, with its subtle sonnet,
gifts a peace that's seldom on it.

Introspective Rustlings

Within the walls of flesh and bone,
 introspection's seed is sown.
 A soft rustle, stirring thought,
 revealing battles to be fought.

 Self-examination's tender shoots,
sprouting questions from the roots.
 Within the rustle, wisdom lies,
 as inner voice becomes the prize.

 Rustlings grow to murmurs loud,
 a solitary mind, unbowed.
 Seeking truths that lie within,
where the deepest dialogues begin.

 The heart's quiet rustlings stir,
 a consciousness begins to blur.
 In reflection, we find might,
 as introspection turns to light.

Feathered Sighs of Stillness

Soft feathers drift in quiet's embrace,
Graceful in the air, a gentle pace.
Silent whispers from a dove's flight,
Stillness courts the soul, pure and bright.

Beneath the sky's vast and endless blue,
Feathered ballet in morning's dew.
Each plumage stroke paints the calm anew,
Serenity's brush, with every hue.

In tranquil moments, wings unfurl,
Sighs of stillness, a silent whirl.
Held in suspension, time's sweet swirl,
Nature's tender kiss, softly unfurls.

Ceaseless echoes are laid to rest,
On zephyrs, the birds are quietly blessed.
Peace ascends as day is undressed,
In feathered sighs, our hearts confess.

Dim Whispers Amongst the Calm

Amidst the hush, soft echoes play,
A subtle breath, the end of day.
Gentle murmurs, the night's refrain,
Whispered secrets in moonlit domain.

Stars above in quiet conversation,
Their dim words spark imagination.
A shared secret with the nocturnal balm,
Translucent threads in the fabric of calm.

The rustling leaves speak low and clear,
Nature's dialect for those who hear.
A cadenced dance unseen in the dark,
Dim whispers that light the spark.

In the stillness what tales are spun,
Tales not for the many, but the one.
A symphony in hushed tones begun,
Suspended in silence, the night is won.

Caress of the Hushed Mind

A hush descends, the mind's retreat,
In quietude, our thoughts meet.
Gentle touch of the serene mind's hand,
A caress in the silent, unseen land.

Adrift in the ocean of inner peace,
Where the torrents of clamor cease.
With each breath, a whispering wind,
Calms the storms that rage within.

In the eye of the mind's tempest still,
The subtle kiss of calm does fill.
Rippling across the mental expanse,
Under the hushed mind's soothing trance.

The velvet night enfolds our care,
In soft repose, we find repair.
Time suspends in tender flight,
In the caress of the mind, a refuge in night.

Tones of Contemplative Winds

Whistling winds through canyons deep,
Carry tales that they sweep.
Contemplative tunes over land they send,
Songs of the earth, in the winds they blend.

Each gust a note in nature's scale,
Harmonies in breezes that dance and wail.
Meditative melodies written in air,
Whispers of wisdom offer their prayer.

Across the meadows, the tones unite,
A symphony of airstreams in flight.
With each puff, a thought is stirred,
Invisible strains, each rightly heard.

So listen close to what they say,
These tones that wander, sprint and sway.
In contemplative thoughts they weave and wind,
Leaving trails of solace for minds to find.

Quieted Thoughts in Repose

In the hush of evening's slumber,
A whisper through the trees,
Gentle wind carries musings,
Of the soul's soft please.

Dreamy skies of velvet night,
Stars twinkle secrets told,
Each a tale of thoughts at peace,
In dusk's calm, they unfold.

Wandering minds find solace here,
In the moon's silent gaze,
Serene their hearts in night's embrace,
The hustle fades, a distant haze.

Slumber wraps its quiet arms,
Embracing day's tired eyes,
In dreams, the mind unwinds and sighs,
Beneath the tranquil, starlit skies.

Subdued Echoes of Self

Reflections stir in muted glow,
Echoes soft and low,
They dance around the mindful shore,
To touch the spirit's core.

The echoes of a life once loud,
Now quiet as the falling shroud,
Subdued beneath the veil of time,
A self-aware, silent chime.

In the hallowed halls of thought,
Whispers of the past are caught,
A gentle reminder of who we are,
A journey traveled, near and far.

The echoes of our inner selves,
Rest on life's dusty shelves,
In quietude, they sing their song,
In silence, we are strong.

Softest Hum of Quietude

A hum beneath the rush of life,
A subtle pulse, a softened strife,
It resonates within, without,
A tranquil mind, no need to shout.

Silken threads of calm intertwine,
A tapestry of peace, design,
The gentle hum, a lullaby,
To soothe the soul, a quiet sigh.

Within the silence, wisdom waits,
As time its hurried step abates,
The softest hum, a trusted friend,
A harmony that will not end.

The din of life grows faint and then,
The hum emerges now and then,
It sings of stillness, sings of ease,
In quietude, the heart finds peace.

Pondering Silence's Song

In silence lies a hidden song,
In quiet corners, all along,
The notes unfold in empty space,
A tranquil, unseen embrace.

The melody of the unsaid,
Floats through the air, in threads of thread,
A symphony without a sound,
In contemplation, it is found.

The rests between the life's loud notes,
Carry the tune that silence wrote,
A peaceful interlude to ponder,
On silence's song, the mind grows fonder.

This song of stillness, soft and clear,
Speaks to the heart when it draws near,
In silence's song, we understand,
The quiet truths that shape our land.

Serenity's Subdued Sentences

Beneath the sky's vast cerulean canvas,
Quietude embroiders its tranquil dance.
Gentle zephyrs scribe in secret glances,
Nature's hush inscribes its subdued expanse.

Whispers weave through willow's weeping branches,
Brooks babble soft sonnets, in silver streams.
Susurrus of leaves, an emerald prance,
Serenity's sentences flow in dreams.

Starlight scripts in silent cosmic stance,
Glossary of glimmer, a nighttime theme.
In the mantle of quiet, thoughts enhance,
Dusky hours hold the most placid gleam.

Hushed horizons blend in a soft whisper,
Day's clamor fades, the night becomes crisper.

Mindful Whispers Among Us

In the hustle, a whisper emerges,
Mindful echoes that softly encourages.
Within the clamor, serenity urges,
Calming the heart as tranquility surges.

Rustling leaves speak, the spirit alights,
The soul's soft murmur, drowned in daylight's tunes.
Between breaths, a quieter voice unites,
Harmonious hush, beneath the moon.

Mind's murmurations, like birds at twilight,
Chattering thoughts hush, peace ascends above.
In stillness, our inner voice takes its flight,
Spreading wings of solace, cradling love.

Guidance whispered, from the depths within us,
Mindful echoes, a soft, connective chorus.

Silence Sings Softly

Silence hums a tune, so faint, so slight,
Harmony's hymn, in the vacuum of noise.
Its melody carries the wings of night,
Softness in sound, its subtle poise.

The unheard chorus of twilight's breath,
Croons to the stars, in twinkling refrain.
Each pause in song, a little death,
Birthing moments, where stillness reigns.

In the hush, a soft crescendo builds,
A choir of calm, in the absence of sound.
Gently it sings, and the heart is filled,
In the silent song, solace is found.

Whispers of the world, barely heard,
In the muted glow, silence sings softly, undeterred.

Shush of Inner Wisdom

In the quietude, wisdom often speaks,
A faint flutter, an inner dialogue.
Hark the hushed voice, when the spirit seeks,
Its muted wisdom, a sanguine monologue.

Gentle shush, within the mind's cathedral,
Softer than a breeze 'gainst the cheek so mild.
With words unwritten, it crafts an ethereal,
A tome of truth, to guide the inner child.

Ears attuned to the subtlest vibration,
Catching the whispers of knowing's breath.
Wrapped in the silence, a calm revelation,
Where sagacity's shush defies death.

Listen close, to the silent intuition,
Therein lies the shush of wisdom's fruition.

Veiled Vespers of the Vigilant

In twilight's hush, the watchful eyes,
Peer through the dusky, deep blue skies,
Guardians draped in night's disguise,
Their silent prayers to stars arise.

Whispering winds through branches weave,
A tapestry that dusk conceives,
Vigilant hearts on quiet eves,
The veiled vespers, the soul perceives.

A solemn oath to keep the peace,
Through shadows' dance and moon's increase,
The vigilant, their watch won't cease,
Till morning's light brings sweet release.

With fervent hope in silent throng,
The night's embrace, they do prolong,
In vespers veiled, they find their song,
And stand together, brave and strong.

Tranquil Whispers of the Waking Dream

In dreams where tranquil whispers flow,
The mind's soft stream begins to glow,
Gentle thoughts, in rhythmic seam,
Weave the fabric of a waking dream.

Beneath the hush of dawn's first light,
An argent world comes into sight,
Where whispers stir the slumbering air,
And peace pervades beyond compare.

A calming breath, a gentle wake,
As life itself begins to quake,
With whispers soft, no need for scream,
We drift between the dream and wake.

This tranquil realm where we convene,
In whispers faint, yet so serene,
A haven safe from day's extreme,
The tender port of waking dream.

Echoes of Stillness

In hollows deep where echoes lie,
The quiet core of earth and sky,
A stillness breathes its silent sigh,
And time itself seems to stand by.

The echoes roam through space so wide,
Where moments rest and thoughts abide,
In stillness, all is amplified,
Each heartbeat marks the slow, hushed tide.

An echo's path, both far and near,
The pulse of silence we can hear,
A symphony so crystal clear,
Resounds within the stillness sheer.

Embrace the calm that echoes bring,
In each quietus, solace cling,
Stillness holds the heart's deep string,
Where echoes soothe, tranquility's wing.

Murmurs Amongst Serenity

A whisper furls in serenity's lap,
Where murmurs rise and then unwrap,
A gentle cadence, a subtle tap,
Like dewdrops on the morning's cap.

Soft murmurings amidst the hush,
As nature paints with twilight's brush,
In tender tones, the world's flush,
Speaks in the silence, time's slow crush.

Each murmur tells of secrets kept,
In serenity's arms, they're adept,
Quiet utterings that have leapt,
From the heart where love has slept.

Listen close to the quietude,
The murmurs speak in interlude,
In the serenity's multitude,
A symphony of solitude.

Zen's Hushed Harmonies

In stillness sits the tranquil mind,
Adrift in silence, peace we find.
The inner hum, a soft tune played,
Beneath life's din, in shade arrayed.

Two-fold the calm, the spirit's song,
With every breath, it floats along.
The pulse of Zen, like a gentle stream,
Flowing unseen, a waking dream.

Petals of thought in wind recline,
Serenity's dance, by design.
Each note that lingers, finely spun,
In hushed harmonies become one.

The quietude, a cloak of calm,
A soothing balm, a whispered psalm.
The heart attuned to softest sighs,
In Zen's embrace, the ego dies.

Peaceful Pulsations

With every pulse, the rush subsides,
In rhythm's lap, serenity abides.
A gentleness suffuses space,
The heartbeat's subtle, soothing grace.

Waves of calm wash over me,
In their ebb, my soul is free.
A tender tempo, calmly set,
In tranquil cadence, worries met.

The steady drum of quietude,
Bestows a patient, peaceful mood.
Life's frantic pace begins to cease,
Giving way to peaceful pulsations of peace.

Soft whispers in the chambered hall,
Each beat a tender, hallowed call.
Echoing in the chest's retreat,
In steady thrum, serenity sweet.

The Breathless Whisper of Being

A silent murmur in the void,
A single breath is thus employed.
In the barest whisper of existence,
Life and being meet at this instance.

The hum of atoms in the air,
The sound of being everywhere.
A voice, a song without a word,
In the breathless whisper, life is heard.

Between each heartbeat's transient pause,
In that space, we find the cause.
The subtle hush of the sacred unseen,
In depths profound, a tranquil scene.

The essence speaks without a sound,
The cosmos in a whisper bound.
In every breath, an echo of the spring,
Where existence murmurs, eternal, serene.

Hush of the Heart's Chamber

In the soft chamber of the chest,
A quiet hush lulls thoughts to rest.
The heart's own chamber, silent, pure,
Keeps secret rhythms, soft and sure.

The hush that folds the soul within,
A sanctuary for what's been.
Emotions ebb, and feelings start,
Cradled in the heart's quiet chamber, apart.

Within the walls that beat and thrum,
A wordless lullaby becomes.
A gentle hush, a pause, a breath,
In love's own hold, a quiet death.

Whispers of longing, soft and sweet,
In the heart's hush, two lovers meet.
The unsaid words, the silent chamber,
A covert place where passions ember.

Unvoiced Vernaculars of Vigil

In silence, the night's own language scribed,
With every shadow, a story imbued,
Moon's soft light on tranquil waters described,
The peace of dusk's embrace silently viewed.

Within the hush, unspoken words do dance,
Each gust of wind, a whisper undeterred,
Crickets' chorus joins in nocturnal trance,
Unvoiced vernaculars so quietly heard.

Under the cloak of evening's subtle shroud,
Secrets told without a sound to the skies,
Stars listen close, they never talk aloud,
Guarding the night with ever watchful eyes.

Vigil held in the quietude of space,
The unuttered tales leave only a trace.

The Intricate Incantation of Stillness

In the still, a silent spell is woven,
An intricate incantation of calm,
Whispered wishes in the air, golden,
Beneath the night's cool, collected balm.

Undisturbed, the world in hushed repose,
Save the soft hum of life's deep undertone,
Time clad in tranquil attire gently flows,
In the quietude, the heart finds its own.

Each leaf's gentle rustle, a secret verse,
A symphony of stillness fills the void,
Nature speaks in tones both clear and terse,
In silent splendors, senses overjoyed.

Stillness weaves its spell till dawn's soft break,
In every silent moment, spirits wake.

Converse with the Quiet

In whispers soft, the quiet converse starts,
The gentle murmur of the slowing heart,
Solitude speaks in a language apart,
In the vast silence, introspections dart.

Words unneeded when the quiet confides,
Each pause more telling than the spoken word,
In the gaps between, true meaning resides,
In silence, the purest thoughts are stirred.

Dialogues with the hush of empty rooms,
Echoes bound within the stillness thrive,
Peace blooms in the space where quiet looms,
In the calm, our inner voice comes alive.

Converse with the quiet, a profound art,
In silence, listen closely to your heart.

Whispers of the Watchful Mind

In the theater of thought, whispers play,
The watchful mind speaks in subtle tones,
Night's dark canvas hosts the words' ballet,
Where shadows weave tales to the unknowns.

Quiet musings fill the air like mist,
Ideas birthed in the depths of the psyche,
Within the mind's maze, they subtly twist,
Whispers paint the corners of thoughts lightly.

Murmurs rise from the well of contemplation,
Reflection's voice, both timid and wise,
A rustling of intellect's conversation,
In the silence, the watchful mind apprises.

Under the hush of a contemplative tide,
Whispers of the watchful mind reside.

Voices of the Void

In darkness deep, where silence dwells,
A realm unseen, where echo swells,
Whispers travel, without a sight,
Voices of the void, in endless night.

Echoes of the absent crowd,
Their murmurs soft, their thoughts aloud,
Incorporal beings converse in code,
In the vast void, their stories unfold.

Spectral words, from lips unseen,
Create a symphony, serene,
A universe of sound, so vast,
Where the present speaks with the past.

The infinite cosmos hums its tune,
In the silent space, 'twixt sun and moon,
A chorus of cosmos, so vivid, so broad,
Voices of the void, in quiet, they laud.

Meditation's Muted Motif

Beneath the mind's tumultuous sea,
Meditation's motif waits patiently,
Softly humming, a melody light,
In the soul's cavern, it shines so bright.

To still the waves of restless thought,
Is the harmony that peace has brought,
Each breath a note, held so dear,
In quiet moments, clarity is near.

Silent sounds from within arise,
Whispery symphony of inner ties,
Gentle rhythm, slow and profound,
Where inner self and truth are found.

Closing eyes to listen in,
Meditation's motif starts to spin,
A silent sonnet for heart's alcove,
In muted tones, it quietly wove.

Calmness in Quiet Whispers

In the hush of evening's fold,
Whispers of calmness, softly told,
In every gentle breath of air,
Serene, the whispers say 'take care'.

The rustle of the leaves in trees,
A murmur in the quiet breeze,
A dialogue without the clamor,
Nature's calm, a soothing hammer.

Hear the silence, golden and pure,
Calmness in whispers, the tranquil cure,
Each quiet swoosh, a tender embrace,
In the softness, find a peaceful grace.

Whispers travel, in silent flight,
Bearing calmness through the night,
In subtle susurrus, they confer,
Serenity's voice, a silent purr.

Subliminal Echoes in the Depth

In the oceanic depths of mind,
Subliminal echoes unconfined,
Vibrations from the deep unseen,
Messages felt but not screened.

Sinking beneath consciousness' layer,
Discover the echoes, hidden player,
A subliminal symphony, quiet and deep,
In the mind's abyss, secrets keep.

Rhythmic pulsating, a silent dance,
From the depth's embrace, echoes advance,
A whispered calling from the core,
Subtle, profound, and wanting more.

Echoes that stir the silent depth,
In the psyche's ocean, holding breadth,
A language of the inner sea,
Subliminal echoes, forever free.

Insights in the Quietude Quilt

In silence's fold my thoughts lie still,
A patchwork of dreams, the quiet does fill,
Each stitch a notion, gently caught,
In the quilt of quietude, insights sought.

Soft whispers of the mind intertwine,
Silken threads in the dusk recline,
Reflection's fabric, seamlessly wrought,
Holding warmth where contemplation is sought.

Underneath the hush, ideas bloom,
Woven deep in the tranquil room,
Sewn with the fibers of peaceful thought,
The quilt safeguards what the soul has sought.

Each square a story, a soft-spoken truth,
Preserved in the quiet, the essence of youth,
Here wisdom nestles, in quietude brought,
In this blanket of quiet, insights are caught.

Hearsay of the Humble Heart

Softly speaks the humble heart,
Whispers of the meek impart,
Gentle are the words it says,
In tender beats, its hearsay lays.

Echoing in the silence, clear,
Truths that only close hearts hear,
Modest in its rhythmic art,
The humble heart reveals its part.

With every pulse, with every throb,
It speaks of love, unveils its sob,
The stories held in gentle red,
In life's loud book, too oft unread.

Hearsay of the heart so mild,
Speaks volumes sweet to nature's child,
In quiet strength, in love's embrace,
The humble heart finds its true grace.

Reverie's Muffled Murmur

In the softness of a daydream's touch,
Reverie's voice whispers as such,
A muffled murmur 'neath the roar,
Of life that races, forever more.

In visions draped in misty hue,
The mind's soft mumblings wander through,
A stream of thoughts, a silent hum,
In the heart's ear, these murmurs come.

A cascade of muted ponderings,
Flow through the mind like gentle springs,
Each droplet, a murmur that stirs,
Within the soul, reverie occurs.

Murmur on, sweet fanciful stream,
In the quietude, let daydreams teem,
For in this hushed and subtle roar,
Lies the peace one's heart yearns for.

Cadence of Calm Curiosities

Curiosities gently knock,
On doors of thought, with tender sock,
The rhythm soft, a calm cadence,
Invites the mind to wide expanse.

In quiet query, whispers rise,
A symphony beneath skies,
Where ideas dance in quiet song,
And calm curiosities belong.

The pulse of wonder softly beats,
In every moment that it greets,
With measured tempo, patient, kind,
It unfolds the treasures of the mind.

Each question marks a tranquil note,
Within the mind's vast sea they float,
In cadence calm, they seek and find,
The answers resting in the mind.

Whispers in Meditation

Annabel Swan

Faint Echoes in the Calm

Beneath the hush of twilight's dim,
Whispers rise on the evening's whim.
Softly treading on shadows' heels,
In the quiet, my heart reveals.

Gentle murmurs of the night's air,
Carrying stories too faint to bear.
Silent echoes traverse the realm,
Guided by starlight's subtle helm.

Echoes dance in the silvered glow,
Rippling through the calm, to and fro.
Serenading the moon's embrace,
Lost in time, in this tranquil space.

Tranquil Conversations Unheard

Leaves rustle with the wind's soft tale,
A silent exchange, beyond the pale.
Branch to branch, their hushed tones spread,
Nature's secrets, quietly said.

The river's babble to the stones,
A discourse in gurgling tones.
To human ears, this speech unheard,
Yet every ripple tells a word.

In morning light, dewdrops confess,
Their fleeting lives, a wordless caress.
Glittering moments on the green,
Tranquil talk, unheard, unseen.

Solace in Solitary Sighs

Alone I find a peaceful ease,
With solitary sighs on the breeze.
No thronging crowd to pierce my shell,
In solitude, my thoughts do dwell.

An inward glance at quiet thoughts,
Tangled threads that time has wrought.
Through the stillness I sift and sort,
Finding peace in the solitude sought.

With each breath's tender pull,
Away from the world's constant lull.
In the silence, my soul unties,
Embraced by solitary skies.

www.ingramcontent.com/pod-product-compliance
Lightning Source LLC
LaVergne TN
LVHW020421070526
838199LV00003B/229